The Fetch

The Fetch

Gregory Leadbetter

Nine
Arches
Press

The Fetch
Gregory Leadbetter

ISBN: 978-1-911027-09-6

Cover artwork: 'Untitled 132' © Eric Lacombe
www.ericlacombe.com

First published October 2016 by:

Nine Arches Press
PO Box 6269
Rugby
CV21 9NL
United Kingdom

www.ninearchespress.com

Printed in Britain by:
The Russell Press Ltd.

Nine Arches Press is supported using public funding by the National Lottery through Arts Council England.

For Freya and Eloise
and in memory of my father
Frederick William Leadbetter

Contents

fetch, *n.*2
1. The apparition, double, or wraith of a living
person

'In this state of mind was comprehended what
is called Poetic Faith before which our common
notions of philosophy give way'

– Samuel Taylor Coleridge

Whisht

Come to this clipping from my hair.
Make a ring of a curl I wore.

I've told you all the truth I know
from the quietus of my pillow.

When I speak your words I feel you
like a wish blown through a candle.

*

Come to this – my bottled breath
warm enough for you to live.

I take up a feather, air-write to you
in magpie black and iridescent blue.

I swallow the pips of an apple core
to grow the godwise food you are.

*

Come to this papercut bleb of my blood
while it is here on my finger to suck.

You know what you have taken from me
better than I have senses to see.

I lay you a trail from a tomb to my door
in photographs, one for each living year.

*

Come to this seed in the palm of my hand.
I've held out my arm as long as I can.

I dry out my sweat, leave you the salt
of my fervid body, torrid or cold.

I set a fire to bring the dawn
and the far imago trying to be born.

*

Come – I've given all you need of me.

Spell out in silence my other name.
I hold my tongue like a flame.

The Fetch

The dream that slammed the bedroom door
but didn't break the film of sleep
to tell the time, or give me more
than broken promises to keep

to phantoms that were never there,
woke me just enough to know
that something was: the restless air,
the waveform of a note too low

to hear, a song to raise the dead.
I listened, and began to speak
as I am speaking now. My breath

condensed. I saw it slowly take
the outline of a child, afraid
of the dark of which it was made.

The Departed

A country road I had driven for years
drawing me into its green lane
bent my car around a corner,
saved my life. I felt a tangent
leave my centre, travel on
into the waiting trees, a heartbeat escaping.

Later, this momentum forgotten,
a word spoken miles away
sat me up in the middle of the night.
My mother told me my great aunt had written
to say she was sure it was me she had seen
crossing a bridge at dawn in New Zealand
while I was asleep in England.

A friend called to say she could swear
it was me she noticed late one evening
leaving a bar in the company of strangers,
laughing, joking in fluent Portuguese.
I looked different, she said, just familiar enough
for her to believe I had learnt a new language.

I was introduced to a friend of a friend
at a party, who stared to the back of my skull
with Black Forest eyes. A bottle of wine
later she whispered, when we were alone,
'You've got a nerve, *du schlechter Mann*,'
smiled a secret, as if I knew what to do
with the number she folded into my hand.

Letters arrived in a child's writing,
always with pictures of a man and a woman
dancing under a crayon rainbow.
I began to leave the post unopened
when the message was always the same,
asking me when I'd come home again.

All this led me to this afternoon,
a séance in a mirror, face to face.
My hands are pressed to the cooling glass,
my eyes are closed in the circle of arms.
A two minute silence adapts my vision
to the breathing darkness. I see
what the part of me that died has seen.

Stalking

Between the fingers of the falling dew
I find a path that takes me through
the sleeping eye to where it wakes
on the other side of the dream it makes

I tread the moss that beds the hoof
I follow into absent proof
a moth without a moon
a wanderer with the day's wound

my fingers are lichen and as slow
my mirror the yew that blisters the shadow

the gift I bring for the darkling birth
is stillness suckled from my breath

I spring the roe   and the world in hiding

Who Put Bella In The Witch Elm

words painted on Hagley Monument, Wychbury Hill

The spelling makes sense when you know
she was found in the yew, folded up
like a foetus put back in the womb,
her knickers soaked with the last
of her voice, a clot in her mouth.

The tree they chose grew
in the lee of a hillfort
fretted with evergreen, top-shelf
magazines if you were lucky,
spirals scored in the bark.

Fire had so hollowed the trunk
that its weight vaulted the empty
space where she was hatched,
where I found wild flowers laid
in a guesswork bouquet of runes.

The Pact

A secret place was all the note said
of where to meet. I chose the woods I walked
the time I lost the key to my house,
returning to find a stranger asleep
on my bed, who woke to say sorry, he got tired
while waiting. Since then I've been writing,
letting the phone ring, dropping my friends.
The work grew like a child between
my daylight hours, a nine-month seal
of shared blood, melted in the wax
of a waning flame that tapered to a scrawl
I knew as mine, telling me *go tonight*.

The figure in liquid silhouette
stepped from the sky between a symmetry
of silver birch, quiet as the morning star.
Held in the split and dawn-red eyes
I felt the kiss of a voice on my throat
sing through my skin with the touch of the air.
I don't know how long I was weightless
in the promise of those words. They
thinned to silence as the sky paled.
I stretched in the darkened sun, mindful
of what would be waiting in my empty house,
whether it would return this greater loss.

Homo Divivus

I found it at the southern fall
  of Clowes Wood – a path I could not walk
without stones in my pockets to carry me
  down past the soft prints
sunk through the clutch of mud and under
  water and our breathing, where
I could not go but they had gone.
  Conditions were perfect:
three days of dry weather, early April
  afternoon, the leaves of oak
still to come. I had the luck
  of the wanderer – woken up
by a thrush trying out all its notes
  as if the combination would unlock
a second sun. I have named the twice-living
  as if they were human,
but they are ultraviolet to visible light.
  What's the use of having found them
except to tell us that we do not know
  the world we inhabit, even when
they are so close, alter the earth
  in ways akin to us, though passing
where we cannot, in sight of what
  we cannot see. They are in hiding
from ignorance – withheld from us
  like plumage on a forest bird
now extinct – a presence whose traces
  move us, whose pattern lives
in other forms: the cuticle of beech
  and the flight between, the circuit

of bine, verdigris lichen, the slant
   tow of sky, the rainbow
sheen that blooms on the marsh,
   their anaerobic speech.
To imagine them is to become
   like them, to haunt a place
as they do – eyes too open,
   amoral as joy. I hear
the hazel buds unfold, listen
   until, like them, I am
diffused, in Clowes Wood,
   a shadow in sound. No more.

Gloaming

It brims from the lake
where a dead fish floats
white as a blind eye.
Some pith of the gloom
hits the back of my throat
with the punch of smoke
no cough can dislodge
so I gulp until its salt
is down to a quiver
of wings in the nest of my lungs.

A grey heron raises the wind.
I hear a mallard mate
with the night at her nape.
The fishermen have left for home
but the conjuring moths
have come. Now I learn
how the bats disappear
through the door of the trees
to return seconds later,
though gone for years.

Lifespan

In the five minutes before it died
without us having realised

we watched an improbable fly –
its tail-antennae, twice the size

of its swivelling body, loop an ankh
from a perfect fork

part again and dowse the air
like a snake's tongue for the presence there –

the peak of its species
in reach for the mote of truth on the breeze –

then buckle under the crush of light,
shrivelled wires the sun had dried.

From the blithe river, other flies
and frequencies rise.

Midsummer at Clent

The year was bleeding across the sky.
I had no voice to give, nothing left
to say anything close to the truth until
I saw the kestrel nailed to the air,
aimed at the sun, holding her zenith
taut on the giddy fulcrum of the earth.
Held up like a lens to a blinding eye,
her feathers suspended in amber.
She stayed near me, as if she were
a periscope over the false horizon.
She stayed until the breath of winter
blew out of the western grave,
freezing a word on the lips of my praise.

Elect

As sudden and as hidden as the turn
of the year in the quickening leaf that pours
from green to green – the law that wakes to learn
the art of transforming effect into cause –

it is our freedom to summon the fact
between the flow of being and the state
of becoming: to know uncertain fate
as a force in concert with our own act.

I've seen the changeling of a chosen power –
a species altered with a thought or word,
its fierce eye the sole witness to the pain –

in a burst of feathers, a plumed flower,
in the present flame of a vanished bird,
nothing's prey: a sparrowhawk, self-ordained.

Sum

When you go and I am
        left to what I am I grope for substance
in the voice I send ahead before I am aware
            that I am heard. I travel the tenses
of my being – what I was, I am, will be – in words
            and I am change itself, a quantum verb
idem et alter in its motion: I am
           because I am a signature in the aether,
marks by type or hand
        that carry what I am beyond my body, at best
the benefaction
that makes it right that I am here, playing the man
  whose first words are *I am*, whose first sight
holds the world entire. I am the man whose many names
remind us we have none. I am the act
that finds and causes what I am: the power to name, to say
            I am is the image of god, my voice
an origin of its own.
   And when you come, I am still the man you know.

This

As if this were unreal, your touch
is more than skin on skin today.

Your voice is more than what you say
although you've never said so much.

There is, I know, a word for this,
or something like it, but it falls short

of knowing what your eyes have taught.
Compare the word 'love' to a kiss.

Accept this gift, an unnamed thing
that does what nothing else can do.

This, the reckless truth we're in
together, of which we are the only clue:

where time is done and we begin,
where you and I are the way through.

Foolslove

Ophrys amor fatui

No world but his had seen him
fall under the hood of her love
in answer to the eye and scent
of all her flower, all the clues
the living are given. Stained
with bliss, he crawls from the bed
of the orchid's mouth, the slick
of her colours on his tongue,
a moon-flake for his halo.

Now, with a look out of mind
as he stumbles after the spore
of his song, as if daylight were dark,
remembering her likeness to a sun
(as if that could be forgotten)
he says (as if the comfort
of something to come) *I slipped.*
And her body was home.

Lessons for a Son

Be still and quiet, so wonderful things
can approach you. A Small Blue may dab
your shoulder, a jay's wing spark through a wood.

Butterflies and birds align you with love
if you look long enough. Keep looking
and they may bring you close to perfection.

Yes, I thought I was an alien too.
You are not alone. (We are not alone.)
True humanity is always a shock.

It is just possible for the whole world
to be wrong. Gravity in fact repels,
for instance. Trust yourself and put the case.

Remember that sex is free, (or should be)
like a conversation. Food and shelter
are there in the landscape, if you look.

The intellect resembles a tool-box;
do not confuse this with intelligence,
which is greater and proves a kind of love.

Thinking is acting. Be careful what you
think, then. The will is a finger pushing
at what happens. Worrying sometimes helps.

Most of all, learn how to learn;
how to be alone, and how to know
when you are ready for your desires.

Do not give up on telepathy.
You are hearing me now, and will have noticed
the overwhelming importance of love.

Statuary I

You become a miraculous thing
when blood soaks through your stone
eyes, slow as wax from the candle
nearby that marks the melting years.

Scabs of lichen bloom across
the bone-stiff drapery of your clothes
like mould on linen damp too long
in the cold of a room without the sun.

I have seen you move in candle-light –
that trick in the flicker of a breath
through flame that makes the livid
brink of perfect stillness dance.

Then, on days like this, you cry.
I daren't dab those tears away.
I watch, instead – remember when
your soft hand took hold of mine.

My Father's Orrery

is without end.
The solar system on the fireplace
spins only one planet around its sun –
Mercury, as if now the limit
of what we know, hints at the missing
planets to come: the ache in the equation
their absence makes, the skewed gravity
at work in the hand that hoped to build
a thing of beauty, week by week,
as the advert said, adding to the stock
of wonder. *Just a con, they are.*
Hasn't he got better things to spend
his money on? But I shared the secret
of his joy in those spheres, his maths
by intuition, the theatre of their relative
motion. He showed me the unopened packets,
the grub screws, nuts and pinions of it all,
and there, the planets themselves:
Jupiter, heavy as antique gold,
the ball bearing Earth, Saturn with its halo.
A look of recognition crossed his eyes –
yes, that's them – but out of orbit,
no force to order and bind them
to the weave of their ellipses,
to turn the key of the space between
and spring them in the cradle of their star,
without which, they rattle and fall.
With the planets in his hands, he felt
the weight of his loss, knew he had forgotten
how to put the universe together.

Dendrites and Axons

I

Rodin's *Thinker* – that was a family myth
for you – *penseroso* in your chair,
the home doctor your in-laws called,
computer-builder, lone cosmographer.
As a child, I could feel you think – see
your eyebrows in the rear-view mirror,
that motorway look – and play at
thinking myself. Now the noise
of what is missing from your mind
crowds and burrs in mine, leaves
no adequate thought for the day's clue:
a photograph of the missing person
I'm going to visit this afternoon.

II

The horse came apart as you drew her –
mismatched perspective, split between the Fuseli head
and something that looked like a pig's rear-end.
This was early enough for a nervous joke
from someone – but though you never said as much,
this was your test, and you knew.

At the hospital, you had to draw a pentagon.
Geometry itself broke open: where
there should have been one, you drew
three, which overlapped like a Venn diagram.

An epicentre in the white space: chaos
in its blossoming fractal.

III

Day and night died too, left you
neither asleep nor awake, but food
for the gut of a corrupted dream.
A body count on fresh-cut grass,
lifeless kids where sparrows should be,
pyjamas on the bed with the dying inside –
the wounded youth who would not survive.

You tried to get out – as if every door
might lead beyond your mind, or back
to the dream of common truth: a marvel
all but lost to you. There was no way out
in fact, but one. You were caught in the glass:
that day you saw your Dad in the mirror
and knew you saw the dead.

IV

The limits not to love
but what love can do: me struck dumb
to find the fact of my love
so wanting in its power to heal, the rage still to come.

The dendrites and axons of love
that bind you to the circuit of the world unravel,
abandon all but love
itself, stubborn and suffering as you buckle.

I want more from love
than love can give, but love does what it can
with earth undone: love
to riffle and raise the dust of the crumbled man.

V

It cannot be done at home.
The walls are open
where they are closed,
closed where they are open.
You fall the stairs, blood
an eye, compress a lung.
It is too much for Mom.

You are here third person.
But just when I think
the man on the sofa
is six months dead,
he wakes, looks and smiles
at me: later, crying,
he calls me his *best boy*

and you are here, Dad, dying.

VI

The first time you didn't seem to know me
even the carers never said hello –
as if they knew I was now a cipher,
a shadow-companion to you.

We move out of synch with the room
like unsteady thieves through a crowd
when Phil, on his way for a smoke
grins over and says *Hello Doctor* –
then sits in the garden, lights up
oblivious. For a moment it's fun
to be not what I am, and I laugh
for the gift – akin to that first lost
Christmas under greyscale skies:
us, going through the motions,
you, buried in the blizzard
of eyes until the new year
sprang in your sudden dance,
that smile forbidding mourning.

You hurry me past Room 13:
It's the Devil. The matter of fact
is subject to change. There are soft
toys stuffed behind handrails
whose cries can be heard all night.
Which one of us cries out for the other
not to go, tearing the air like paper?
The goodbye that we haven't yet had,
the goodbye that we are in.
What's your name now? It has vanished
into its component sounds, its other
language, watchful as that woman

in the corner with her hands around her ankles
and eyes black as dabs of tar
that swallow what's left of the light.
Your questions continue to arrive.
You recognise a fellow ghost
in me, and ask *What killed you?*

Back home, mirrors imagine me
alive. I seek consolation
in a splash of water – look up
to see the face washed from me.

VII

Consider Taylor's *Holy Dying*:
it is a great art to die well

but you were denied the archaic wish
of a studied death, patient
as your body was those final hours,
breath and pulse and little more.
Dying was the last thing
you could learn: the loss came first,
left us only its scarce resource.
My philosophical refinements,
& metaphysical Theories
lay by me in the hour of anguish,
as toys by the bedside
of a Child deadly-sick.

I get the call that says to come
over a hundred miles away.
The hours tighten at the approach –
twisted oaks throw down their leaves
through waving woods on rain-damp roads
the clocks put back, as if to bring
me to you at the cost of light.

Keep your eyes dry you said out of nowhere
that once. Was that the riddled wisdom
you'd laid down without a word
being spoken? There was something else:
Live so as to leave a good ghost.
That was years ago, in contemplation,
your mind your own, or borrowed

from this time, the shadow-fall
of prophecy. I arrive to find you
in its beam – endings crushed
to a stop, still enough
to close on, to kiss.

It is warm, this dying, lit through
by the leaves of the lamp
in the corner of the room.
The lamp is a tree, this night
its season. I am not fit
to speak, though I let
words fall as they will:
Always be travelling well
with you almost gone
Always be travelling well
as I hold your hand
Always be travelling well
as I let go.

I will not breathe with you
again once I leave.
I stand in the doorway, as if
to enter, and you were a child: echo
of your goodnight shadow
when I turn to sleep.

VIII

You are too still for mind to bear – so that
I see your chest rise, only to catch on the fact
that I have not, like a foot on a missing stair.

I listen, but a star has blown and a black hole
drags the howling air to the density of silence.
Everything happens out of sight.

The door to the dead room is closed.
I touch and take the shock
of your skin. No sound escapes its cold.

Pumpkin

The black bloom of mould
that crept through the eye
of the carved head, between
his death and funeral, within a week
of the flame that gave the glow
and shiver of life at Hallowe'en
to shadows dying into smoke –
black soot that clings, carries
hollowed flesh to pale filament,
spores of air – holds my gaze
with the blind pupil it has grown.

Feather

Here is the feather that knocked me down
that dead-sky morning, no other trace
of the wing it lifted from the ground

but the swan-stark remnant that I found,
which gave its colour to my face.
Here is the feather that knocked me down.

There's knowledge we don't know we carry around.
I can only hold this feather displaced
from the wing it lifted from the ground.

It left me with nothing that day but the sound
of my blood beating into empty space.
Here is the feather that knocked me down.

My father is not so old as I am now.
This feather's perfection cannot replace
the wing it lifted from the ground.

But there's enough in its vane of barbs to astound
his absence, just enough fragmented grace
to find in the feather that knocked me down
the wing that lifts me from the ground.

Doggerland

Mesolithic

This is the tide of the earth's tilting,
of years too long before, too far ahead
for thoughts tied to the daily sun,
the closed grip or gift of seasons – of utmost
memory, and beyond that, myth, animal-shapes
known to speech but never seen.

Today the past returns as water,
drowns the future with last summer's camp.
No rush for now, only the need for higher ground
and new words for that distant feeling
as they sat, warm and dry, looking down
over the blue plain, bereaved.

White Horse Hill

Snowed with ghosts
and the freezing glow
of the sky lowering
its hushing light

the pastures close
cool and cotton
over England's
buried names.

A grey witness
goes into the land,
inhumes the day
inside its clues.

The trees stretch,
tell the time,
stow the trace
of a distant gun.

Renewing

Come with me, this time
　　where the wind is farmed
　　　　without a sound from where I stand

and try to catch a silent power
　　on the wing, as they do – where
　　　　the cliff-rock scrolls inscrutable law

dreamt in the snort and sleep of depth
　　that sounds in the sea-mouths
　　　　under my feet, where I find the brink

of a setting sun and wear its rainbow
　　parhelion, and catch the cliff-path in my stride
　　　　to Beeny, past the sudden bullock's brow

that meets mine at the stile where the berries
　　aren't yet sweet, but pregnant like that eye
　　　　with ocean swells, the vandal squall that rises

now and blows the sea into my hearing
　　in light that parts the valley's gash and teeters
　　　　me out past the fantasy of solid ground

along the edge in time to enter
　　the throat of the sun as it glisters
　　　　on the split of the sheer rock-drop

where I catch the tread of the air, at last
　　this song my bridge and my stair.

Misterioso

A shell at my ear,
I heard the whisper of my heart's work:
I fell open like a book.
I watched the quiet of the moth's flight,
drawn to silence like the moth to light:
the life within the one we hear.

Now I am the instrument that I play
and I am played by the sound
I make: remade by the touch of the air,
by the rhythm and note of what I say –
as if the world is something I have found
and the world knows that I am there.

And if the best of speech is music – a sense between
the skin and something understood –
returns the tongue
to its own song,
gives the blood
its dream

let its language

bring us close
to the first of us: the cave of eyes
lit by the fire of what they heard –
the drum that gives the ghost
its dance: the voice that swells the earth
like fruit: the cry that carries on the listening skies.

Sea Change

Don't be afraid. Step over the edge. You'll fall; don't try to fly. Arrow yourself like a pelican; think fish. Sight yourself beneath the surface; know that your first gulp of the sea will swallow you whole. Feel your skin silver as you plash headfirst into your element. Dive. Leave the shallow reach of the air where it left you, and the sky you no longer need to fill the hollow bones of gulls. Now remember. Let the lost gills behind your ears breathe again, your flesh fill with water. The sinking light will expand your eyes, inflate them to a gape for the sun. Slip out of your hands and feet and swim. Smooth your shoulders, merge your legs. Your spine will thread you to the current. Think squid. Go deeper. Descale yourself as you cool into the dark. Mould yourself to the tide, reabsorb your architecture. Pale as you grow monstrous, a creature to tangle sperm whales in the drowning tentacles that leap from your head. Taste the oceans at their tips. Trust your seeing tongues as your eyes widen into blindness. Distil the ink of your blood. Listen for the lowered waves, tectonic cracks travelling through sunken storms, the filaments of voice resounding depth on depth. Slow now to the rhythms of sleep. Shrink into the dust of life that resists the flattening miles above. Think polyp. Your eyes will close into the pulp of senses. Drag the sea-bed to the caustic plume of a thermal vent, spewing grains of the molten source, the liquor of mountains. Anchor at the mouth of its boiling pore and spread your fronds. Be still. Begin to feed from your beginning.

The Leap

Devonian Period

Something not yet thought
wakes out to sea,

breaks through the shoal as they turn
and plate the current.

We're unrecognisable
in their ache to spawn:

the tug of warmth that tempts
them to the surface,

the dare of something not yet
hope, the tide-route

that takes them as far as the shore
not yet knowledge,

the need to shake their young
into the fresh water

beyond the parched bridge
of land, survival.

Something not yet fear, more
than the barely-begun

singularity in the gills that will
snatch at the air

in the seconds spent crushed
by the sun: waiting

skeleton-first in the crackle
of light, the giant

scorpion takes its shape,
the sudden darkness

remembered now, as something
not yet human

rushes

Arcadia

Don't go to the real Arcadia
looking for Pan or the gods in leaf.
The sun has dried the earth for weeks,
buried its water. The cypresses stake
their green on the dust and the scrub
clings to the cracked hillside and waits.
The olives grow fat on memory alone.

Remember the island you left to make
this journey. Its soil is still in the tread
of your shoes. The wind in the trees is the sea
you crossed. Return through the vulva-scent
of the hawthorn: a fresh lung of light
brings out the rock and grass like rain,
lifts the skullcap of the moon-by-day
and shows him, naked as the olive stone:

a man-child with the head of a ram,
his brain a womb with Fallopian horns.

Bat-Light

exists between
the veil of azure
and the cool oil
of ultramarine

where what has fled
in place of sight
has wings of skin
the cave has bred

and sounds beyond
all human speech
that fasten the living
and free the dead

True Story

I knew a child who became unwell.
She'd found it difficult to play
for a while – then one day
couldn't move when she fell.

For all the watchful bedside hours,
for all the sudden flowers,
for all they wish they never knew,
even a parent needs to sleep.
Her mother dreamt of her blue-eyed girl
wandering the corridor
but in between what she could keep
she lost her at the hospital.
She cried all her tears, and lost those too.

Later that week, her silent husband
spoke. *She's here,* he said,
I found this at the door.
He held a gift bag, and inside
was a doll.
Her pale skin was loosely stitched
as if she never had been whole.
Her foam heart was an open wound,
her left hand a clenched fist.

They dressed her in her favourite pink,
and quietly put her to bed.
Sleepless, staring, they lay by her side.
Just before dawn, they saw her blink.

Baby Monitor

At the nudge of a shadow, the lamp
is lit – the empty house
to the would-be thief: *I'm home.*

The kettle's cold, everything
unplugged – all but the fridge
with its chuckle and hum

and the baby monitor
left on: a fizz in the air
from the bedroom to the lounge.

At a certain hour, the lamp
goes out, and a sound
comes feeling for the light –

the speaker downstairs
is breathing – very gently
tells the darkness: *I'm awake.*

Masts

The air is not itself today:
it can no longer rest. The last
free molecule has just been put to use.

Our alpha-waves are butterfly-brained.
Sleep, in any normal sense,
has not been possible here for months.

I carry an egg for safety now.
I came too close the other day:
it cooked in my pocket, good enough to eat.

The Astronaut's Return

She looks familiar; yes, she is my wife.
Her hair is longer; it's been months.
I don't think she expected to see me again.
She doesn't talk as much as I remember
and when she does she's speaking to a child.

I notice how her body moves beneath her clothes
and when she's naked, in the bath or in bed,
how independent it is, in spite of her.
When she sees me looking she turns away.
When I touch her skin she flinches.

The clothes she says are mine no longer fit.
Eat, she says, *please eat*, and *I love you*.
I soothe her as best I can. I tell her that
I'm learning to come back. But my eyes,
still wide open, sparkle like topaz when I sleep.

The Chase

I bought him a drink for all the old times
and prepared for an evening over his shoulder.
From a distance I saw his life as a comedy,
laughed at the anguish that ran through his face
as he caught himself at it again: chasing
the hare through the eyes of strangers, exhausting
himself on a scent that led him a dance.

I felt the air shift when she came towards him.
As if marked by a sign, they were a pair
before they knew it. I gave them my blessing.
He followed her as she slipped into him.
I watched them talk and saw it running
between them, its eyes there in a glance
then gone, its ears alert to the hunt.

They felt its heartbeat flutter in theirs,
sure they had it caught, though I knew better.
He kissed her, as if for the first time
feeling for proof in her lips and her skin,
innocent of the hare cocked for the leap
back to the wild: when he looked in her eyes
I saw my reflection double and run.

The Body in the Well

Even here, where the aquifers are spoken of
with a reverence strangers save for cathedrals,
it's rare to find a house like this, three stories
of gleaming limestone raised like a lantern
out of the rock, lit like a match when struck
by the stone of the clear moon, a pale flame.

The locals say the house was a dream of his,
climbing like a pyramid month on month:
building it was a way to forget. *Make
this dream your own*, the auction-catalogue
tells the buying public. *The property
includes a well* follows in a quieter font.

He would listen at the mouth in the floor
of the cellar, patient for the voice of the dark
in the sound of the stalagmites rising.
When he fell into its echoing heart
the waters gathered him with their song
and here, he remembered everything.

Statuary II

Your laughter is overgrown
and silent too – there are no
birds in this damned wood,
and no path – only you.
I should not have come.

More rotten stump than stone
but for the grey brow
at knee-height – a satyr's head.
Moss has stuffed your mouth,
gifted you a sphagnum tongue.

Without your own,
the wood's your laughter now.
I am just the latest joke.
I see a sudden jackdaw land
before it laughs out loud.

The Hollow

Follow the shrinking path to take you
curving through the slopes of light, the trees
that close the gate behind you. Your feet
tread heavily at first as the earth
takes time to remember you. Move
so the birds know it's a child's footstep
they can hear. Listen for Rachel's voice, she'll call
any moment now, drop you a trail of daisies. Here's
the house she called the castle, the blown-out
windows you climbed through. Leave what you found
there one midsummer undisturbed today. You were told
never go into the woods alone, even with Rachel
at the promise of a kiss. Follow her voice
in the blackbird's alarm. The path is one child
wide now. Push past the nettles that stung her thighs
and your hands as you tried to stop them. The dead
tree shoulders from the undergrowth, years ago
stripped by a ribbon of light. Rachel
tells you she will kiss you. It was here.

Descent

Wondering how gardens grow
has led me to this: hands
green at last with the stain
of fruitless strawberry, a fork

in the earth and the turn
of my arm, nerves in the tines,
eyeless with the worms
in the shift and slither under sound,

the sun at my back and the natter
of the birds so close
at my shoulder, startled
into song as roots come clear

like nothing I've known:
soft bones, headless and hollow,
my fingers blackened and damp
with their touch, the fork in the ground

suddenly finding its note

Deadheading

The rose winters inside itself
below the tide-mark of last year's growth

and its first gifts to the slow spring
are the withered crowns where flowers had been

and I arrive in my dream season
marked and woken by that tension

knowing I am one more sign
the curious god that walks the garden

I pare each stem with the pinch of a law
that couples the dead with the yet to be born

making way for plight and blossom
eyes still blind with earth to open

and when the sun falls on my neck
and severs my head from the morning air

it frees in the twofold tips of my fingers
a human bud, murmuring leaves

Clairvoyance

To be awake is to keep
one breath back unbreathed:
the weight of daylight,

the bird in the rib-and-gristle
cage whose flitting brings
this interval of sight,

a travelling back in time,
the universe returning
to pool in the cup of the skull.

A hush, and this is sleep:
wings folded, finch-hops to the edge.

The body sinks, one breath lighter.
Scales tip into the dark future
with the weight of one bird, singing.

Black-Necked Grebe

They say it escaped from a cunning-man's coop,
dived into air one midwinter and left him
without spell or sight – to live unseen
in its own season behind the wind and water,
waiting for the right crack of light to make
its crystal feather – the black and rufous thing you see.

I once came close. Heard its whistle shear
off into the world that dogs can hear –
that brings them running or drives them mad.
What I'd give for a gold quill dropped
from its head, or what the old man heard it whisper.
On the Fal, in cold weather, they come to pan for its eyes.

Peregrine

On its branch of bone defleshed
by lightning, dinosaur-limb,
transmitter of that starving cry
stolen from a fossil's throat,

hinge of fallen jaws that gape
a ravine and rust in sandstone
split and slaked by the North Esk,
swallowing the sun the trees digest

and re-forge as the ring and crown
of the falcon's eye, the jet fulcrum
of the gorse-gold talon, the limpid trance
in which it holds and strips the sky –

stoops to grip and pick
and mantle death, spit its feathers
from the nest, fan its matter
into barb and flight

to which its prey is magnetised.
I still train my voice for when
without a sound the peregrine comes
familiar to my flayed hand.

Gibbet Lane

Cut the rune on the hanged man's tongue

and he will speak –
eat the days with you,
give your eyes the glare
that sees where light is blind
but every truth intact.

He hangs from the tree
by the umbilical noose of his own birth –
fruit of the coursing life
of the dead, the teeming dark
where the brain takes root.

The human travels out of human shape
in his fluent decay,
chewed by babbling mouths
into what we are without ourselves –
water stripped to the fire of its elements.

He breathes where the living lose their breath
and gods dissolve with flesh.
His acid-sweet odour is an open flower
to the speech you send beyond itself
to take its nectar – speak beyond our nature.

His lips move with your own.
Your question is his consummation
and his crime. The knowledge
taut at the hanged man's neck
chokes on its own utterance

as he cuts the rune on your tongue.

Mirror Trick

You didn't have to say the Lord's Prayer
backwards for the Devil or your true self
to appear: only hold your own stare
in a mirror long enough and he would come.
The Ouija season, those mid-teens, a game
of being, and of our tuck shop myths, this one
hinted at some half-insight of folk intelligence:
an experiment for an empty house at night.
The trick was not to blink: only then
would the circuit hold and the surface
deepen with the reach of light. I have lived
some portion of my future since I saw
that figure form itself from what I am
in what was left of my reflection, a sealed
dimension in the silvering: a priest-hole
for something other than a priest to hide
in plain sight. Released, I knew him by those eyes
like mine, become at once too dark, too bright.

Imp

On the bad days, I shooed her mews away
out of nothing but an absence of joy.
I never installed a back-door flap for her,
so she would patter all night to get in at the window
while I lay wide-eyed and sleepless, pretending not to hear.

I know it was a blessing
when she landed like a fly on my forehead
as I was trying to write,
her cicada rustle scribbling in and out
before the flick of my hand sent her to hide
in the plumbing, where she whined for weeks
until I found her, toad-shy and morning-blind
in the kitchen sink. I held her, for the first time then,
revived her with what has become her favourite wine.

It has often been her game
to go missing. It is where she thrives,
as if she delights in being imagined –
looked-for in the fading light,
or at the beck of a buzzard's call.
In the garden, I would find her spraint,
stinking of rotten fruit and putrid grain,
the tang of iron and the fume of honeycomb.
She would announce her return with a black-out
bite through electrical cable, then creep in close, dab
my eye with a spider-leg to see if I was awake.

She could drive me mad
with her cuckoo blink –
then I remember how she would
pull me out of the O of a dream
when I couldn't breathe
and make me a day-bed from her sloughed skin.
She would lap at whatever saltwater
leaked from me. It wasn't right
for her to see me cry,
but she would tongue my tears away,
curl me a rabbit-fur snake
for a pillow and blow through my ears.
Her opalescent gaze could break
the world-egg open
over and over again.

Tonight, I will leave out a bowl
of blood and marrow to tempt her back,
fall asleep on the sofa, wait
for a child's hand to touch my face.

Cradle

The bog is a beating fontanelle
at the place I cast a penny wish

where carr and fen leaches out
an orphaned head for the fallen sun.

Lowered, severed, through this depth
of thickened spring, drowned leaves
from every heaven there has ever been

a glut of kohl that runs with rain down
the pouring face

sunk to stop its singing, to stop its crying
but still it cried, when no one came.

Too late for fright at who it is,
the kisses lost on blackened lips,
the mother and father

whose ghosts cannot bear to look
at what has become of flesh
that outlives ritual, run to seed
so powerful

mouth and eyes as closed to mind as bone
but for the dark rhizome
fruiting through their foetal sleep

the lit nerve that crazes the earth,
the skull its pale mineral.

Soft and pulsing now,
drawn like water from a spawning well
it is the foundling head I bring

that thinks the wish that wishing
grows a thing through which
my tongue might leave its lair.

There's no one here
but me between the sensory trees
and the ecstasy that exceeds its birth

as I sink a voice to a singing head,
as a white hand bursts from a limb of ash.

Notes

Whisht

whisht, *n.* 1. An utterance of 'whisht!' to enjoin silence
2. Silence.
3. A whisper; with negative = 'not a whisper', not the least utterance.
adj. Silent, quiet, still, hushed.
v. 1. To be silent, keep silence.
2. To put to silence, silence, hush.

wisht or **whisht,** *adj.*
2. Uncanny, eerie, weird

wishtness, *n.*
Melancholy; something uncanny or supernatural
(*Oxford English Dictionary*)

The Fetch

See epigraph, and:

fetch, *n.* 1. 1a. The action of fetching, bringing from a distance, or reaching after; a long stretch, a far-reaching effort.
2. A contrivance, dodge, stratagem, trick.
4. An indrawn breath, a sigh.
(*Oxford English Dictionary*)

The Departed

du schlechter Mann (German): 'you naughty man'.

Homo Divivus

The name, in scientific taxonomy, for the species described in this poem: 'twice-living' or 'double-living' human.

Sum

Sum (Latin): 'I am'.

idem et alter (Latin): 'The same and the other' – among other things, an echo of Coleridge's description of the self-differentiating principle of the Logos ('Word' and/or 'Reason'), the 'communicative Intelligence, Natural, Human, and Divine'. Coleridge in turn draws upon the philosophical theology of Philo of Alexandria (c. 15 BCE–c. 50 CE).

'the power to name, to say / *I am* is the image of god': see Exodus 3:14 ('I AM THAT I AM').

Foolslove

'Foolslove' is the folk or common name – and contracted translation – for the orchid whose botanical name is *ophrys amor fatui*.

Dendrites and Axons

Dendrites and axons are the communicative relays of neurons ('input' and 'output', respectively).

I – *penseroso* (Italian): Meditative, thoughtful; brooding, melancholy.

VII – 'It is a great art to die well' is from Jeremy Taylor, *The Rule and Exercises of Holy Dying* (1651); 'My philosophical refinements . . . a Child deadly-sick' is from a letter of S.T. Coleridge (1796), which reworks a phrase he had read in Taylor's *Holy Dying*, and copied into his notebook.

Doggerland

The area of land now under the North Sea that once connected Britain to the rest of continental Europe. Rising sea levels eventually flooded this landscape during the Mesolithic period (c. 9600 BCE–c. 4000 BCE). Britain became an island around 6000 BCE.

Misterioso

Italian, used in a printed score as a musical direction as to how to play: 'mysterious' or 'mysteriously'.

The Leap

The Devonian Period describes the period of earth's natural history between c. 419 and c. 359 million years ago. Palaeontological evidence suggests that it was during the later stages of this period that fish first moved on land, and the link evolved between fish and the first air-breathing, land-dwelling vertebrates.

Imp

The word 'imp' derives from the Old English *impa/impe*, meaning 'bud, shoot, scion, graft, child'.

Acknowledgements

Acknowledgements are due to the editors of the following publications in which some of these poems, or versions of them, have appeared: *And Other Poems, Birdbook II* (Sidekick Books, 2012), *CAST: The Poetry Business Book of New Contemporary Poets* (Smith/Doorstop, 2014), *Heaventree New Poets 4* (Heaventree Press, 2006), *Magma, The North, Poetry London, The Poetry Review, The Rialto.* Seven of the poems here were published in the pamphlet *The Body in the Well* (HappenStance, 2007). 'The Astronaut's Return' was highly commended in the Arvon International Poetry Competition 2004. 'The Chase' was shortlisted for the Strokestown International Poetry Competition 2005. 'Sea Change' (with different lineation to the present version) won Third Prize in the RSPB/*Rialto* Nature Poetry Competition 2012. 'Misterioso' was commissioned by Birmingham City University to commemorate the tenth anniversary of the Music for Youth National Festival at Symphony Hall, Birmingham, in 2014. '*Sum*' was commissioned by Writing West Midlands for BBC Radio 4, 'Something Understood', and broadcast on 12 April 2015. I am grateful for a Hawthornden Fellowship in 2013, during which several of these poems were written.

My warm thanks go to the friends and family that have helped me to bring this book into being – in particular, to my tutors at Goldsmiths in 2003-04, Maurice Riordan, Stephen Knight and Maura Dooley; to Jane Commane; to Helena Nelson, Lawrence Sail and Alison Brackenbury for their early encouragement; to my wife, Karen, for all her support; and to Sally Read and Jonathan Davidson, for conversations past, present and continuing.